● soho
● theatre company HOUSE

Michael White
in association with Soho Theatre Company and Richard Jordan present
the West Yorkshire Playhouse production

SMOKING WITH LULU

by **Janet Munsil**

First performed at the Courtyard Theatre, West Yorkshire Playhouse
on 3 November 2000.

Performances in the Lorenz Auditorium

The play is a work of fiction inspired by the actual meeting of Kenneth
Tynan and Louise Brooks in 1978, and Tynan's subsequent New Yorker
Magazine Profile, 'The Girl in the Black Helmet', published in 1979. The
author acknowledges indebtedness to the writings of both Brooks and
Tynan, and to numerous biographical sources.

Smoking With Lulu was first produced as *Emphysema (A Love Story)*
by Alberta Theatre Projects, D. Michael Dobbin Producing Director, as
part of Pancanadian playRites 1997.

 THE ARTS COUNCIL OF ENGLAND   LONDON ARTS   SUPPORTED BY CITY OF WESTMINSTER

Soho Theatre is supported by

 gettyimages   **A&B** Arts & Business NEW PARTNERS   **Bloomberg**

The **Guardian**   TBWA\GGT DIRECT

Registered Charity No: 267234

SMOKING WITH LULU

by **Janet Munsil**

Louise Brooks	Thelma Barlow
Kenneth Tynan	Peter Eyre
Lulu/Librarian's Voice	Sophie Millett

Director	David Giles
Designer	Kenneth Mellor
Lighting Designer	Michael Odam
Sound and Video	Mic Pool
Choreographic Consultant	Stephen Mear

Production Manager	Nick Ferguson
Stage Manager	Lorraine Tozer
Deputy Stage Manager	Andrea Gray
Chief Technician	Nick Blount
Production Electrician	Sebastian Barraclough
Scenery built and painted by	West Yorkshire Playhouse
Costume Supervisor	Amy Brown

The production would like to thank:
Lyn and Albert Fuss
Atlantic-Film SA (for film extracts from *Pandora's Box* 1928)
Elspeth Cochrane
Olivia Harris (Personal Assistant to Michael White).

Press Representation
Angela Dias at Soho Theatre (020 7478 0142)

Advertising
Haymarket Advertising for Guy Chapman Associates

Graphic Design
Jane Harper

Publicity Photography
Keith Pattison

Soho Theatre and Writers' Centre
21 Dean Street
London W1D 3NE
Admin: 020 7287 5060
Fax: 020 7287 5061
Box Office: 020 7478 0100
Email: box@sohotheatre.com
www.sohotheatre.com

THE COMPANY

Cast

Thelma Barlow Louise Brooks

Favourite theatre roles include: Madame Ranevsky in *The Cherry Orchard* (Bristol Old Vic); Mam in Alan Bennett's *Enjoy* and Madame Arcati in Noel Coward's *Blithe Spirit* (West Yorkshire Playhouse). Thelma appeared as Mavis Wilton in *Coronation Street* (1973-1997). Recent TV credits include: *Call My Bluff*, *Murder Most Horrid*, *David Copperfield*, *Dinnerladies* (BBC); *Fat Friends* (ITV) and *Simply Gardening* (Carlton TV). Radio credits include *Nemesis*, *Sunny Side Up* and the not-yet-broadcast *A Surfeit of Lampreys* (all BBC Radio 4). The film *King's Ransom* also awaits release.

Peter Eyre Kenneth Tynan

Peter made his stage debut with the Old Vic Company and did repertory seasons in Harrogate, Glasgow, Birmingham and two years in Nottingham where he played Edgar in *King Lear* (also at Old Vic) and the Prince in *The Idiot*. He played Konstantin in *The Seagull* (Chichester Festival and Greenwich Theatre); Oswald in *Ghosts*, Hamlet in *Hamlet* (Greenwich Theatre); Axel in *Comrades*, Tim in *The Desert Air*, Toulon in *Red Noses* (RSC); Tesman in *Hedda Gabler* (RSC Aldwych also Australia, USA and Canada); Tusenbach in *The Three Sisters* (Cambridge Theatre); Ferdininda in *A Country Life*, Ronnie in *The Potsdam Quartet* (Lyric Hammersmith); Antiochus in *Berenice*, Pyrrhus in *Andromache*, Edgar in *King Lear* (Old Vic); Brunelli in *The Madman of the Balconies* (Gate Theatre); Polonius in *Hamlet* (Almeida and Broadway); *Chere Maitre* (Almeida and Flea Theatre, New York); Ken in *Smoking with Lulu* (West Yorkshire Playhouse). TV includes: *Momento Mori* (BBC); *The Two Mrs Grenvilles* (Lorimar); *Friends* (Warner Bros); *Midsommer Murders* (Bentley Productions); *Don Quixote*, *Alice in Wonderland* (Hallmark) and *Bertie and Elizabeth* (Carlton). Films include: *Maurice*; *Let Him Have It*; *Orlando*; *Surviving Picasso*; *The Golden Bowl*; *From Hell* and *The Affair of the Necklace*. As director: *Bajazet* (Almeida); *Siblings* (Lyric Hammersmith) and his own version of the Flaubert – Genge Sand correspondence with Irene Worth, *Chere Maitre* (New York, London, Melbourne Arts Festival). Concert appearances include: *Midsummer Nights Dream*, *Le Bourgeois Gentilhomme* (London Mozart Players); *A Soldiers Tale* (LSO); *Britten/Auden Theatre* pieces (BBC singers at the Aldeburgh Festival)

Sophie Millett Lulu/Librarian's Voice

Graduated from the Royal Scottish Academy of Music and Drama with a BA (Hons) and prior to this trained at the Bush Davies School. Theatre credits include: *Smoking With Lulu* (West Yorkshire Playhouse); *Barefoot in the Park* (Royal Northampton)*; The Importance of Being Earnest* (West

End) and *Sweeney Todd* (Bridewell Theatre). Television includes: *Taggart*, *McCallum* (STV) and *Bernard's Watch* (Carlton). Film includes: *High Heels and Low Lifes*; *Mr Ma and Son*; *Longitude* and *The Biographer*.

Company

David Giles Director

Trained as an actor at the Northern Theatre School and as a Television Director at the BBC. As Artistic Director at Lyric Hammersmith (1979-1981) credits include: *You Never Can Tell*, *Country Life*, *Hobson's Choice* and *The Potsdam Quartet*. Other theatre includes: *'Tis Pity She's a Whore*, *The Wood Demon* (The Actors' Company); *The Young Idea* (Yvonne Arnaud Theatre); *Lies and Gigi* (West End); *On Approval* (touring); *Twelfth Night*, *Measure for Measure* (Stratford Ontario, Canada) and *The Waltz of the Toreadors* (Shore Theatre, Niagra-on-the-Lake, Canada). American Theatre includes: *The Country Wife*; Edward Bond's *Lear* and *Antony and Cleopatra* (Dallas Shakespeare Festival). Television includes: *The Darling Buds of May*; *The Forsyte Saga*; *The Mayor of Casterbridge*; BAFTA nominated *Barchester Chronicles*; *Mansfield Park*; *A Murder is Announced*; *Resurrection*; *Vanity Fair*, *The Strauss Family*; *On Approval*; *The Winslow Boy*; *Sense and Sensibility*; *Richard II*; *Henry IV Parts 1 and 2*, *Henry V*; *King John* (Shakespeare series, BBC); *Fame is the Spur*, *The London Embassy*; *The Fools on the Hill*; *Forever Green*; *The Bill* and *The Gospels*. David directed many episodes of *Hetty Wainthropp Investigates* and in 1995 he directed two series of *Just William*. Film includes: *Dance of Death* (with Laurence Olivier); *Hamlet* (Ian McKellen); *Nicholas and Alexandra* (Dialogue Director for Sam Spiegel) and *A Murder is Announced*. David has also taught for 10 years at RADA.

Richard Jordan Co-Producer

Trained in Stage Management at the Oxford School of Drama and the Cameron Mackintosh Chair of Drama at St.Catherines College, Oxford. Previously produced at Soho Theatre: *Rum and Vodka & The Good Thief*. Other productions and co-productions include: *St.Nicholas* (Assembly Rooms, Edinburgh); *Rum and Vodka & The Good Thief* (Citizens Theatre, CBB Theatre Sao Paulo, Brazil, and tour); *Gods Official* (Everyman and Unity Theatres, Liverpool and tour); *Kissing Sid James* (Octagon, Bolton); *Sweeney Todd – the Demon Barber of Fleet Street* (Bridewell); *After the Fair* (King's Head); *Almost Forever But* (Assembly Rooms, Edinburgh); *Anna Weiss* (Whitehall Theatre); *Troilus and Cressida* (Old Vic); *Of Thee I Sing* (Bridewell); *Shylock* (Hampstead and tour). He is a consultant for Teatros.Art, Brazil's largest chain of independently owned theatres. In 2000 he became one of the first recipients of the TIF/SOLT New Producers Bursary Awards.

Kenneth Mellor Designer

Kenneth's career has combined design in architecture, television and theatre. Trained and worked as an architect in Yorkshire, he then ran a group of designers for the Greater London Council producing exhibitions, graphics and colour and light schemes for the Thames Bridges. Theatre design with director David Giles: *The York Mystery Plays*; *The Word Demon*, *Tis Pity She's A Whore*, *The Phantom of the Opera* (with the original Actors Company); *You Never Can Tell*, *Country Life* and *Hobson's Choice* (Lyric Hammersmith); *The Young Idea*, *On Approval* (Guildford); *The Waltz of the Toreadors*, *Measure for Measure (*Canada); Rossini's *Elizabetta d'Inghilterra and Elizabeth the Queen* (Holland). For Ronald Eyre: *Hobson's Choice;* for Anthony Quale: *Rules of the Game*; for Lindsay Anderson: *The Cherry Orchard* (Theatre Royal Haymarket); for Robert Chetwyn: Ustinov's *Beethoven's Tenth* (Vaudeville and New York); *Eastward Ho!* (Mermaid); *Luv* (Amsterdam) and for Maria Aitkin: *After the Ball* (Old Vic). Most recently *Smoking with Lulu* and *Blithe Spirit* (West Yorkshire Playhouse).

Janet Munsil Writer

Janet Munsil lives in Victoria, British Columbia, Canada. She is a graduate of the University of Victoria Theatre Programme. Since 1992, she has been the Producer of the Victoria Fringe Theatre Festival and the UNO Festival of Solo Performance. Her plays include *The Ugly Duchess* and *Be Still.* Her published children's books include *Where There's Smoke* (Annick Press) and the award-winning *Dinner at Auntie Rose's* (UK edition, Oxford Press). *Smoking With Lulu* was her first full-length play, originally produced in Canada under the title *Emphysema (A Love Story)*.

Stephen Mear Choreographic Consultant

Stephen trained at the London Studio Centre. Stephen's recent credits include: *Smoking With Lulu* (West Yorkshire Playhouse); *Singin' in the Rain* (West Yorkshire Playhouse and Royal National Theatre); *The Witches of Eastwick* (co-choreographer Theatre Royal, Drury Lane); *Of Thee I Sing* (Bridewell Theatre) and *Soul Train* (Victoria Palace, West End) which earned him an Olivier Award nomination. Television includes: *Monster Café, Hangar 17* and *Megamaths* (all for Children's BBC).

Michael Odam Lighting Designer

Recent productions include: *Bouncers* (Churchill Theatre and tour); *Saturday Night Fever* (for Joop van den Ende, Holland); *Singin' in the Rain* (Royal National Theatre); *Dr Livingstone I Presume?* (Riverside Studios); *Smoking with Lulu*, *Blithe Spirit* (West Yorkshire Playhouse); *Smoky Joe's Café* (regional tour); *The Rocky Horror Show* (Birmingham Rep and national tour); Richard O'Brian's musical *Disgracefully Yours* (London and New York); *Great Expectations* and the 21st anniversary of *The Rocky Horror Show* (West End and European tour). As Associate Lighting Designer relighting includes: *The Phantom of the Opera*; *Joseph and the Amazing Technicolour Dreamcoat* and *Carmen Jones* (all for the Really Useful Group, national and international tours). Other theatre credits include: *Fame*, *Anything Goes*, *Aspects of Love*, *Les Miserables*, *Time* (West End); *Guys and Dolls* (London and Australia); *Kiss Me Kate*, *Follies*, *Song & Dance* (London and European tour); *Bugsy Malone*, *42nd Street* and *My Fair Lady* (London and Toronto).

Mic Pool Sound and Video Design

Mic has been resident at the Lyric Theatre Hammersmith, Royal Court Theatre, Tyne Theatre Company and toured internationally with Ballet Rambert. He has designed the sound for two hundred productions including more than one hundred for the West Yorkshire Playhouse where he is currently Director of Creative Technology. In 1992 he won a TMA award for the sound design for *Life Is A Dream*. He was nominated for a Drama Desk award for outstanding sound design 2000 for the New York production of *The Unexpected Man*. Video work for theatre includes *Singin' in the Rain* (West Yorkshire Playhouse, RNT and National Tour); *The Taming of the Shrew* (RSC); *Rinaldo* (Grange Park Opera); *Rakes Progress*, *The Turk In Italy*, *Il Trovatore* (ENO); *Johnson Over Jordan*, *Dangerous Corner* (also West End), *Smoking With Lulu*, *Half a Sixpence* (West Yorkshire Playhouse); *Das Rheingold* (New National Theatre Tokyo). Television includes the sound design for *How Wide Is Your Sky* (Real Life Productions for Channel Four).

Michael White Excecutive Producer

Michael began working in the theatre at the White Barn, Connecticut as Assistant to Producer Lucille Lortel and returned to London to become Personal Assistant to Sir Peter Daubeny. Some of his productions include *The Connection* by Jack Gelber, *The Secret of the World*, *The Voice of Shem*, *Son of Oblomov*, *Loot*, *The Burglar*, *The Beard*, *Soldiers*, *The Resistible Rise of Arturo Ui*, *So What About Love*, *Sleuth*, *Yoko Ono*, *Bluebeard*, *Hamlet*, *The Dirtiest Show in Town*, *As Time Goes By*, *Entertaining Mr Sloane*, *What the Butler Saw*, *Pina Bausch*, *Housewife Superstar*, *Dracula*, *Deathtrap*, *Jackie Mason*, *Me and Mamie O'Rourke* and *Boys in the Band*. Musicals include: *Oh, Calcutta!*, *Dancin'*, *The Threepenny Opera*, *Joseph and the Amazing Technicolour Dreamcoat*, *The Rocky Horror Show*, *A Chorus Line*, *Annie*, *Ain't Misbehavin'*, *Y*, *The Pirates of Penzance*, *Metropolis*, *She Loves Me*, *Crazy For You*, *Fame*, *The Musical*, *Voyeurz*, Disney's *Beauty and the Beast* and *Notre Dame de Paris*.

Janet Munsil on *Smoking With Lulu*

When I was fourteen, I bought a bundle of fifty or so old *New Yorker* magazines at a rummage sale. There was a fair distance between the coastal British Columbia logging town I lived in and anything remotely cosmopolitan, and I clung to the magazines like a life-raft. I memorized the theatre listings in the 'Goings on About Town' department, already a year or more out of date. And through reading and rereading his theatre reviews and celebrity profiles, I fell in love with the *New Yorker*'s drama critic, Kenneth Tynan.

'The Girl in the Black Helmet', Tynan's lengthy *New Yorker* profile about the enigmatic silent film siren Louise Brooks, had all the makings of a lovely and unhealthy fairy tale. Both had been seduced by elegant self-destruction, both were haunted by the immortal film image of the amoral Lulu in *Pandora's Box*. I was touched by the transparency of Tynan's worshipful love for Brooks, and was unsettled when his idol began to reciprocate.

Fifteen years later, I was having a post-show chat with an elderly theatre patron, who was bemoaning cigarette smoking on stage in that evening's production of *Private Lives*. (Since then, smoking in any public place has been banned in many Canadian cities – including on stage.) 'Can't they just mime it? Without terrible smoke? Couldn't someone invent a little white straw that glows in the dark?' Just then, I though of Lulu, suspended in air. A wisp of smoke, listening, laughing, changing shape.

● soho
● theatre company

Soho Theatre and Writers' Centre
21 Dean Street, London W1D 3NE
Admin: 020 7287 5060 Fax: 020 7287 5061
Box Office: 020 7478 0100 minicom: 020 7478 0136
www.sohotheatre.com   email: box@sohotheatre.com

Gordon's

Bars and Restaurant
The main theatre bar is located in Café Lazeez Brasserie on the Ground
Floor. The Gordon's® Terrace serves Gordon's® Gin and Tonic and a range
of soft drinks and wine. Reservations for the Café Lazeez restaurant can
be made on 020 7434 9393.

Mailing List: Join our FREE mailing list by contacting the Box Office on
020 7478 0100 or email us at box@sohotheatre.com for regular online
information. Annual membership of the postal mailing list costs £10;
cheques should be made payable to Soho Theatre Company, with your
name and address on the back of the cheque.

Hiring the theatre: Soho Theatre has a range of rooms and spaces for
hire. Please contact the theatre managers on 020 7287 5060 or email
hires@sohotheatre.com for further details.

Also at Soho Theatre late night comedy:

6 – 23 February (Weds–Sat only): Catherine Tate, 8pm and Julian Fox in
Rebranding Mr God, 9.15pm. 'Phenomenal… destined for greatness.'
The Sunday Times on Catherine Tate; 'Perfect late night entertainment.'
The List **** on Julian Fox

28 February – 2 March, 7 – 9 March: Julia Morris, Show and Tell.
'Induces helpless, giggling joy that leaves you weeping for more.'
Metro*****

28 February – 1 March: Roger McGough, Everyday Eclipses.
'The patron saint of poetry' Carol Ann Duffy

13-16 March: Live! Girls!
'Exceptionally funny and perceptive character based comedy' *Daily
Telegraph*

19 – 22 & 26 – 30 March: Barb Jungr's Every Grain of Sand
'A wonderful singer and a soulful diva who really knows how to work
an audience.' *The Sunday Times*

Coming up

25 – 26 February and 4 – 5 March: St Nicholas by Conor McPherson
with Peter Dineen from TV's Father Ted.

April – June 2002: Touring Season
UK's brightest and most innovative touring theatre companies come to
Soho for the first time. Line-up includes: Graeae; Frantic Assembly;
Unlimited; Actors Touring Company; Paines Plough and Traverse Theatre
Company.

Soho Theatre Company

Artistic Director: Abigail Morris
Assistant to Artistic Director: Sarah Addison
Administrative Producer: Mark Godfrey
Assistant to Administrative Producer: Tim Whitehead
Literary Manager: Ruth Little
Literary Officer: Jo Ingham
Associate Directors: Jonathan Lloyd, Tessa Walker (trainee)
Director of Writers' Programme: Lin Coghlan (part-time)
Development Director: Carole Winter
Development Manager: Kate Mitchell
Development Officer: Gayle Rogers
Press Officer: Angela Dias (020 7478 0142)
Marketing Consultant: Isabelle Sporidis
Marketing Officer: Ruth Waters
General Manager: Catherine Thornborrow
Front of House and Building Manager: Anne Mosley
Financial Controller: Kevin Dunn
Finance Assistant: Hakim Oreagba
Box Office Manager: Kate Truefitt
Box Office Assistant: Steve Lock
Box Office Assistants (Part-time): Steven Egan, Leah Read, Michael Wagg, Barry Wilson
Duty Manager: Mike Owen
Front of House: Sarah Benson, Morag Brownlie, Sharon Degen, Claire Fowler, Sarah Gurcel, Harpreet Kauz, Sam Laydon, Helen Le Bohec, Rob Mayes, Joanna Potts, Claire Townend, Kellie Willson, Annabel Wood and Jamie Zubair.
Production Manager: Nick Ferguson
Chief Technician: Nick Blount
Technicians: Sebastian Barraclough and Adrian Peterkin
Board of Directors and Members of the Company: David Aukin *chair,* Cllr Robert Davis *vice chair,* Lisa Bryer, Tony Elliott, Barbara Follett MP, Norma Heyman, Bruce Hyman, Lynne Kirwin, Tony Marchant, Michael Naughton, David Pelham, Michael Pennington, Philippe Sands, Eric H. Senat, Meera Syal, Marc Vlessing, Zoe Wanamaker, Richard Wilson OBE, Roger Wingate,
Honorary Patrons: Bob Hoskins *president*, Peter Brook CBE, Simon Callow, Sir Richard Eyre
Development Committee: Bruce Hyman *co-chair*, Catherine Fehler *co-chair*, Philippe Sands *vice chair*, Nicholas Allott, David Aukin, Don Black OBE, David Day, Amanda Eliasch, Emma Freud, Madeleine Hamel, Norma Heyman, Cathy Ingram, Roger Jospé, Jonathan Lane, Lise Mayer, Michael Naughton, Barbara Stone, Richard Wilson OBE, Jerry Zimmermann.

THE SOHO THEATRE DEVELOPMENT CAMPAIGN

Soho Theatre Company receives core funding from Westminster City Council and London Arts. However, in order to provide as diverse a programme as possible and expand our audience development and outreach work, we rely upon additional support. Many projects are only made possible by donations from trusts, foundations and individuals and corporate involvement.

All our major sponsors share a common commitment to developing new areas of activity with the arts and with the assistance of Arts and Business New Partners, encouraging a creative partnership with the sponsors and their employees. This translates into special ticket offers, creative writing workshops, innovative PR campaigns and hospitality events.

The **New Voices** annual membership scheme is for people who care about new writing and the future of theatre. There are various levels to suit all – for further information, please visit our website at www.sohotheatre.com/newvoices

Our new **Studio Seats** campaign is to raise money and support for the vital and unique work that goes on behind the scenes at Soho Theatre. Alongside reading and assessing over 2000 scripts a year, we also work intensively with writers through workshops, showcases, writers' discussion nights and rehearsed readings. For only £300 you can take a seat in the Education and Development Studio to support this crucial work.

If you would like to help, or have any questions, please contact the development department on 020 7287 5060 or at development@sohotheatre.com

We are immensely grateful to all of our sponsors and donors for their support and commitment.

West Yorkshire Playhouse

^{WY}**PLAY HOUSE**

Since opening in 1990, the West Yorkshire Playhouse has established a reputation both nationally and internationally as one of Britain's most exciting and active producing theatres, winning awards for everything from its productions to its customer service. The Playhouse provides both a thriving focal point for the communities of West Yorkshire and theatre of the highest standard for audiences throughout the region and beyond. It produces up to 16 of its own shows each year in its two auditoria and stages over 1,000 performances, workshops, readings and community events, watched by over 250,000 people. The Playhouse regularly tours its productions around Britain and abroad.

Alongside its work on stage the Playhouse has an expansive and groundbreaking programme of education and community initiatives. As well as a busy foyer and restaurant which are home to a range of activities through the week, the Playhouse offers extensive and innovative education programmes for children and adults, a wide range of unique community projects and is engaged in the development of culturally diverse art and artists. It is this 'Arts for All' environment, as well as a high profile portfolio of international theatre, new writing for the stage and major productions with leading artists that has kept the Playhouse constantly in the headlines and at the forefront of the arts scene. Artistic Director Jude Kelly is a leading and visionary spokesperson for the arts, proving through the work of the Playhouse how theatre can play a critical role in society and the creative economy.

For West Yorkshire Playhouse

Jude Kelly Artistic Director (Chief Executive)
Maggie Saxon Managing Director (Company Secretary)
Ian Brown Associate Artistic Director
Paul Crewes Producer
Diane Asken Company Manager
Daniel Bates Director of Corporate Affairs
Helen Child Theatre Manager
Rachel Coles Head of Press
Suzi Cubbage Production Manager
Caroline Harrison Finance Director
Kay Magson Casting Director
Sam Perkins Head of Arts Development Unit
Mic Pool Associate Director, Creative Technology
Kate Sanderson Marketing Director

West Yorkshire Playhouse
Playhouse Square
Quarry Hill
Leeds LS2 7UP
www.wyp.org.uk

First published in 2002 by Oberon Books Ltd.
(incorporating Absolute Classics)
521 Caledonian Road, London N7 9RH
Tel: 020 7607 3637 / Fax: 020 7607 3629

e-mail: oberon.books@btinternet.com

A catalogue record for this book is available from the British
Library.

ISBN: 1 84002 284 1

Cover photograph: Keith Pattison

Cover design: Oberon Books

Printed in Great Britain by Antony Rowe Ltd, Reading.

Characters

KEN

LULU

LOUISE

Projections

Title slides and film clips should be projected on the
back wall behind playing area, the title slides' type
styles and borders suggesting silent film titles. Film
clips should be edited to remove titles and additional
characters, or for time; for details please contact the
playwright's agent.

Smoking With Lulu was first performed under the title *Emphysema (A Love Story)* by Alberta Theatre Projects, D. Michael Dobbin, Producing Director, as part of Pancanadian playRites 1997, at the Martha Cohen Theatre, Calgary, on 5 February 1997 with the following cast:

KEN, David Schurmann

LULU, Ravonna Dow

LOUISE, Shelia Moore

Director, Micheline Chevrier

Set Designer, Helen Jarvis

Costume Designer, Judith Bowden

Composer, Alan Rae

Lighting Designer, Brian Pincott

Stage Manager, Colin McCracken

Assistant Stage Manager, Gina Moe

Smoking With Lulu is a work of fiction inspired by the actual meeting of Kenneth Tynan and Louise Brooks in 1978, and Tynan's subsequent *New Yorker* Magazine Profile, 'The Girl in the Black Helmet', published in 1979.

The stage is divided into three areas. A black projection screen hangs above for slide and film projections.

Upstage right is LOUISE's room. A bed, a nightstand with telephone, and later, a kitchen chair. No real doors or windows.

Upstage left, an elevated area where LULU makes her appearances, with steps leading downstage.

Downstage left, a large ottoman draped in black satin, and a standing art deco ashtray. This is KEN's area, where he is joined by LULU as indicated.

In blackout, a cigarette is lit. Spot up slowly on KEN, standing. He takes a drag and exhales, watching the smoke in the stage light. He has a stutter which he uses to great effect.

KEN: There is no piece of stage business more brilliant than this. Nothing more personal. Nothing more sexual. There is nothing more elegant, more indifferent, nothing that draws the eyes to the beautiful hand, the sensual mouth, the hypnotic gaze, the breath made manifest. The lifting to one's lips, the element of fire, the suck, the burn, the glowing ember, the excruciating eternity before the pleasure, the climax, the sigh, the ashes.

Takes another drag to illustrate.

It is a kiss blown off the edge of the stage and out into the dark that says 'fuck you, darlings.' I know you're out there. But you are nothing to me. Look at you, watching me. At this moment, I am your entire world.

And another, taking his time.

I'm creating atmosphere.

And another.

I'm making you *wait* for me. How can you help but fall in love with the curl of smoke above my head? Soon it will reach out to you, a tender and illicit lover. Is it secretly touching you now? Is it stroking your face, your eyes, caressing the rim of your nostril? The wraith that haunts you now has been deep inside my body, inside my lungs. It was, for one breath, the air I breathed. My inspiration.

Inspire. (*He inhales.*)

Expire. (*He exhales.*)

Salvador Dali told me that his ideal erotic experience would involve two people whose sexual responses were so acute that they could stand at opposite ends of a huge baronial hall, dressed in shrouds with only slits for the eyes, and by looking at each other in a certain way achieve orgasm. I suppose if one could get an actress to look at an audience like that, that would be *it*. But we still have *this* moment together. Where I can touch you, without touching you.

Title slides appear with the following captions: 'Smoking With Lulu', 'with', 'Kenneth Tynan', 'and', 'Louise Brooks'.

Lights change to LOUISE in bed, smoking and surrounded by books and papers. She is writing rapidly and crossing things out. Something blocks her train of thought and she picks up the phone on her bedside table and dials a number she knows by heart.

VOICE: (*Off.*) Rochester Public Library. (*Pause.*) Hello?

LOUISE: Is this the Rochester Public Library?

VOICE: (*Off.*) Yes it is, ma'am.

LOUISE: I was wondering if you could tell me how one spells 'catastrophe'?

VOICE: (*Off.*) Catastrophe. C, A, T, A, S, T, R, O, P, H, E. (*Pause.*) Ma'am? Did you get that? Hello?

LOUISE: (*Writing it down.*) Yes. Thank you darling.

She continues to write as she hangs up the phone. She picks up the phone again and dials.

VOICE: (*Off.*) Rochester Public Library.

LOUISE: How do you spell 'catastrophe' again?

VOICE: (*Off.*) Is this Miss Brooks?

LOUISE: Fuck off.

She hangs up and goes back to writing. Phone rings.

Oh, what! What! What! (*Picks up the phone.*) Who's this?

VOICE: (*Off.*) This is the Rochester Public Library, Miss Brooks.

LOUISE: How did you get my number?

VOICE: (*Off.*) Miss Brooks, it has come to our attention that books taken out in your name have been returned to the library in a condition that we consider unacceptable.

LOUISE: Will you get on with it? I'm a sick old woman and you're wasting the last few precious moments of my life.

VOICE: (*Off.*) Miss Brooks, we have to ask you to stop making corrections in the film history books you borrow.

LOUISE: Are you calling me a vandal?

VOICE: (*Off.*) We ask that you respect the books we send you if you wish to retain your borrowing privileges.

LOUISE: Privilege? To read that garbage?

VOICE: (*Off.*) Miss Brooks, I need to inform you that this is a circulating library. The books must circulate. But when you write notes and corrections in the margins of our film history books, and people recognise the marginalia as yours, they steal the books.

LOUISE: Well, maybe they recognise the truth.

VOICE: (*Off.*) Miss Brooks, these thieves are not film historians. Our film section has been decimated.

LOUISE: Decimated. Decimated?

VOICE: (*Off.*) Yes. It means…

LOUISE: Of course I know what decimated means, you idiot. Do you know what it means?

VOICE: (*Off.*) Well, yes.

LOUISE: I don't think you do, darling.

VOICE: (*Off.*) Miss Brooks…

LOUISE: It means to select every tenth man for punishment. And that is something that I know something about, you pretentious little shit.

VOICE: (*Off.*) I'm sure you've had a fascinating life, Miss Brooks. I read Kenneth Tynan's profile of you in the *New Yorker.*

LOUISE: So I guess you think you know me pretty well. I guess you think you know me well enough to tell me how to behave.

VOICE: (*Off.*) It was a wonderful tribute to you, Miss Brooks. I thought about you when I read his obituary last month.

LOUISE is silent.

(*Off.*) Are you still there, Miss Brooks?

LOUISE: Bastard.

VOICE: (*Off.*) I'm sorry?

LOUISE: What did it say about him?

VOICE: (*Off.*) The obituary? He had emphysema. He was fifty-three. He said an indecent word on live television.

LOUISE: Anything else?

VOICE: (*Off.*) Well, he was a drama critic. And that sex show, *Oh, Calcutta!,* that was his.

LOUISE: That's it?

VOICE: (*Off.*) I can look it up for you and send you a copy.

LOUISE hangs up. Pause. She picks up the phone again and dials.

(*Off.*) Rochest...

LOUISE: How do you spell decimated?

VOICE: (*Off.*) Miss Brooks, I have to ask you to stop calling every...

LOUISE: Spell it!

VOICE: (*Off.*) D, E, C, I, M, A, T, E, D.

LOUISE: Thanks, darling. (*She hangs up.*)

Lights fade. The opening credits of 'Pandora's Box' are projected, leading up to Lulu's entrance. Lights up on KEN. He watches the film.

KEN: None of this would have happened if I'd not noticed in my TV Guide that at one p.m. on a sunny afternoon I could view a film on which my fantasies had fed since I first saw it, a quarter of a century before. I wondered how many of my Santa Monican neighbours would be lured away from a poolside brunch to watch a silent picture, shot in Berlin in 1928. The story of an artless young hedonist who, meaning no harm, rewards herself and her lovers with the prize of violent death. Lulu.

He turns back to the film and watches silently for a moment as, in the film, Lulu pours the Meter Man a drink.

I think of the scene in Citizen Kane, when Bernstein tells the story of how, in his youth, he saw the girl in the white dress for an instant, from a distance, and not a month goes by that he doesn't think of that girl.

LULU enters upstage. She is dressed like the screen Lulu, a bottle tucked under her arm.

Look at her. *Look* at her. (*He continues to watch the screen.*) She wears beaded dresses in the afternoon, sips cocktails in a Library Bar where only men go, where the light is always Manhattan in the first week of November, four-thirty p.m. In my childhood dream of my life in the adult world, she is my heroine. Aristocratic, sophisticated, cosmopolitan. And so *modern.*

LULU sits and parts her robe slightly, extending her leg to straighten a black stocking.

LULU: Darling.

KEN: She's mine. (*Still watching the film.*) She is bound to every fantasy, to every erotic notion, to the very idea of sex, bound hand and foot to the bedpost with a silk stocking. The heathen idol in my religion.

LULU: Darling?

KEN: Darling.

LULU: Come on, darling.

He hesitates.

Come on. Have a drink, darling?

KEN: Of course. Was someone here? Before me?

22

LULU: (*Pouring his drink and handing him a glass.*) Just the man who reads the meter. Bottoms up, darling.

KEN: Who?

LULU: The delivery boy.

KEN: And?

LULU: The milkman, the cameraman, the stuntman…

KEN: Rapacious harlot.

LULU: Oh, darling, I'm a tramp, not a whore.

KEN: You have been a very naughty little girl, Lulu. You'll have to be punished.

LULU: No! No!

KEN: A wicked little vixen.

LULU: No!

KEN: Take that off.

LULU: I won't! (*She drops her robe. Underneath, she is wearing complicated erotic underwear, garters etc.*)

KEN: Down.

LULU: I won't! I won't!

She throws herself down and he spanks her while she shrieks.

No! Help! Have mercy on me! Pity me! You…you…

The film shows the theatre scene with Schoen in the props room. Actors synchronize with film action for the rest of the scene. LULU pounds the pillow with her fist, shakes her head from side to side, and kicks her legs in a very erotically charged and self-conscious temper tantrum, looking up occasionally to see what effect she's having.

KEN: Oh, but I do, you despicable hoyden.

He sits next to her, simultaneous with Schoen in the film, shaking his head. He begins to laugh at her display. She sees this and becomes angry, sits up and pounds him with her fists. They grapple, and kiss. They are interrupted by Alwa and Schoen's fiancée. LULU looks up and smiles mischievously.

(*To audience.*) You see…

LULU searches though his pockets for a cigarette like a child looking for candy. When she finds his cigarette case she opens it and takes a cigarette greedily.

LULU: Do you have a light, darling?

KEN: (*Lighting her cigarette.*) …She is a ruinous cobra, but she fascinates.

LULU: Thanks, darling. (*Exits.*)

KEN lights his own cigarette and sits alone for a moment.

KEN: Dear Miss Brooks.

A title slide appears:

Rochester, New York

LOUISE enters. She sits on the bed and reads a letter as KEN speaks.

KEN: Dear Miss Brooks. You probably don't know me, but I am an English author and drama critic, and former Literary Manager of the National Theatre of Great Britain. Last year I moved to the U.S.A. to work for The *New Yorker*, and write a series of articles about people whom I admire. I recently saw *Pandora's Box* for a third time and my admiration for you was instantly rekindled.

LULU is revealed in the background, scantily clad as before. Her arms are over her head. Her wrists and mouth are bound with wide black patent leather straps

I am interested in meeting you at your home in Rochester to discuss your life and films for a profile.

LULU begins to fidget.

When I remarked to my editor that I had an interest in you…

LULU: (*From behind her gag.*) Darling?

KEN: Hm?

LULU: (*Pulls down her gag.*) How much longer?

KEN: In a moment.

LULU pulls up her gag again.

…I was pleasantly surprised when he told me that you were still living. Living in New York, and that you had published a number of brilliant articles on your film experiences and the people you worked with in Hollywood and Berlin. I would like to meet with you at your home in Rochester in late April. If we could spend two or three sessions talking about your fascinating life, I would be very…

LULU whines for attention.

Shut up a moment, will you darling? I do so look forward to the opportunity of meeting you. Yours sincerely. Kenneth Tynan.

(*To audience.*) You'll excuse us.

(*To LULU.*) You bad thing!

Lights change to LOUISE, in bed, who reads over the letter she has written in reply.

LOUISE: Dear Mr Tynan. I am writing this fast and mailing it fast so I won't be able to take it back. I usually mark unfamiliar correspondence 'deceased'. So sorry to disappoint you, but I have none of the qualities you've assigned to her flickering self on the screen. And as for a lengthy *New Yorker* profile, I don't know if there's a person on this earth that I couldn't sum up in a thousand words. So the answer is no.

LOUISE is distracted by the sound of a garbage truck pulling up outside.

Regards, Louise Brooks. P.S. As for knowing who you are, Mr Tynan. I know. And I believe you are a very naughty boy.

A few loud crashes and honks interrupt her.

What the hell is going on out there? (*Crossing to her window.*) What the hell is going on? What are you doing? Is that necessary? Don't you have any respect for a person's right to a little peace?

A metal trash can and lid are thrown and roll down the street.

Pick that up! You pick that up! Don't you dare leave, you bastard!

Truck drives away.

You pick that up! Bastard.

She turns back to her letter and adds a further postscript.

P.P.S. If you must come, bring a gun.

Lights change.

A photo slide appears: a portrait of Louise with a long strand of pearls. KEN appears in light, rehearsing their meeting.

Title slide:

Rehearsal

KEN: Darling! Darling. Oh, hello darling. Louise. Darling Louise. Miss Brooks. Darling.

Lights up on LULU, posing as in the photograph, with a single floor-length strand of pearls looped over her outstretched hand.

LULU: Darling!

KEN: Darling, you look darling, darling.

LULU: Darling, you are a *darling* to say so.

KEN: Drink, darling?

LULU: Of course, darling. (*She produces glasses and a bottle, and he pours.*) Oh darling, I have waited all my life for this moment.

KEN: I suppose you have. (*He raises his glass.*) To you.

LULU: To you.

KEN: Oh, darling, oh *one,* let us often, that is to say, *always*, read the same books.

LULU: Oh, daaaaaaarling.

KEN: We shall have brilliant conversation. Here is a list for you of essential reading.

LULU: *Communist Manifesto, The Necessity of Art, Tynan on Tynan.*

KEN: I will bring out everything that is possible in you. But you will never come to me with your troubles.

LULU: Never, darling. I understand completely.

KEN: I should tell you that I have unusual sexual tastes.

LULU: Darling?

KEN: I like to spank girls. Are you *terribly* shocked?

LULU: Why no, darling.

KEN: Then you must worship me plainly. You must dress as I tell you. I shall take lovely photographs of you looking terrifically European.

LULU: I can't allow that.

KEN: Whyever not, darling?

LULU: Because when you take my picture you steal my soul, darling.

KEN: Then we must be seen together always. Laughing, fighting.

LULU: Let there always be something going *on* between us.

KEN: Suspicion, jealousy, intrigue, sudden meetings.

LULU: Let us pretend not to care.

KEN: Let us lose touch with each other for months.

LULU: Years! Let us forget each other completely.

KEN: When we forget each other, we shall cease to exist.

LULU: Forget me quickly, darling, I beg you.

KEN: I can't darling. There's a curse on you. Now that I've seen you I cannot ever *undo* seeing you. Ever since I first looked upon your wonderful and incomparable beauty, I have dared to love you wildly, passionately, devotedly, hopelessly.

LULU: Oh, darling.

KEN: I hope I shall not offend you if I state quite frankly and openly that you seem to me to be in every way the visible personification of absolute perfection.

LULU: I think your frankness does you great credit, Earnest. If you will allow me, I will copy your remarks into my diary.

KEN: Oh, stop.

LULU: What, darling?

KEN: Stop, stop.

LULU: Why?

KEN: This is *The Importance of Being Earnest*. We're doing *The Importance of Being Earnest*.

LULU: Oh. (*Pause.*) Do you want to tie me up, then?

KEN: Maybe later.

Lights change. Title slide:

Dorothy

LOUISE is lying in bed, smoking, several books, articles, research lying around her. She is reading a copy of Tynan's 'Curtains'. LOUISE flips over the book to study Ken's picture. A knock at the door.

LOUISE: I don't want any!

Eventually a knock.

(*Shouting.*) I don't want any I said.

KEN: (*Offstage, stammering.*) It's me. It's Ken. Miss Brooks. I know I'm a bit early. Your neighbour let me up. I could come back later.

LOUISE: Just a minute. Just a minute. Just a minute, I'll be right there.

KEN is dressed for outdoors in a long black coat, scarf, gloves. Bottle of wine, leather bag.

KEN: Ah, (*He has a coughing fit.*) hello. It's me.

LOUISE: You're too early.

KEN: I'm very sorry. (*Coughs.*) Excuse me. I hope It's not too inconvenient. If you're busy I can come back…

LOUISE: So you're the illustrious Kenneth Tynan, hm?

KEN: Yes.

LOUISE: You're different than I imagined.

KEN: Oh?

LOUISE: I've been reading your books.

KEN: Oh, I see.

LOUISE: You're different than I thought. In real life, you don't look so…

KEN: Young?

LOUISE: Intelligent. You look too…hmmm, wicked. Like a satyr.

KEN: How marvellous.

LOUISE: I never imagined that you'd have a… (*She waves vaguely at her lips.*)

KEN: Oh, the, uh, stammer. You hardly notice it when I write.

LOUISE: I hope I didn't offend you.

KEN: No, of course not.

LOUISE: I think it's gorgeous.

KEN: It rarely bothers me these days. When I'm upset or excited. Nervous.

LOUISE: Are you nervous now?

KEN: (*Laughs.*) Yes, I'm very nervous.

LOUISE: Good. Well, come in, this place is a dump.

KEN: Not at all.

LOUISE: I bet I'm not quite what you had in mind.

KEN: Oh, no, really, yes.

LOUISE: Liar.

KEN: Yes. Well, I must say this is a very great pleasure…
I brought you a bottle… 'Fifty-nine Burgundy. Supposed
to be a very good year.

LOUISE: I wouldn't know. I was drunk that year.

KEN: Oh. (*Alarmed.*) Do you not…then you don't…?

LOUISE: What the hell. It's a special occasion. It's a party
compared with the rest of my life.

KEN: Ha.

Pause.

LOUISE: Well.

KEN: Yes?

LOUISE: Are you waiting for the sun to cross over the
yard arm?

KEN: Oh, pah. Shall I? I'll look after this, shall I?

LOUISE: Give it to me. I'll do it. (*As she exits, making circles
in the air with her finger.*) Where's your goddam thingy?
The thingy is over there. (*Makes plugging-in gesture.*)

KEN: Tape recorder? No, I don't have one.

*LOUISE enters with open bottle and plastic tumblers. KEN
pours, swirls his wine in the tumbler, holds it up to the light.*

LOUISE: Bottoms up.

KEN: I suppose we should get started.

LOUISE: I'm desperately tired.

KEN: I could come back tomorrow.

LOUISE: Might as well get it over now that you're here.

*LOUISE starts to get into bed. She is having some trouble
and KEN doesn't know if he should help.*

KEN: Here, let me…

LOUISE: (*Pointing to the tray table.*) Just get that out of the way.

KEN: Here okay?

LOUISE: Thanks, sweetie. (*She picks up the book.*) Sign it. Not for me. For Marge. She's my upstairs neighbour. I'd be dead if it weren't for her. Brings me three meals a day, doesn't ask for a dime. She's a darling and I'm just wicked to her, just wicked. I can't help it. She's one of those caring, concerned types that you want to, oh, kick.

KEN: Is she interested in the theatre?

LOUISE: No. She's interested in famous people.

KEN: I see.

LOUISE: She's never heard of you.

KEN: Well, that's fine.

LOUISE: I didn't tell her about your *Oh, Calcutta!,* or that you're the man who said 'fuck' on live TV.

KEN: Yes. My epitaph.

As he hands the book to her, his attention is caught by Louise's shoes. She notices KEN staring at them.

LOUISE: Is there a problem with my shoes?

KEN: I'm sorry.

LOUISE: Space shoes.

KEN: I'm sure they're very comfortable, darling.

LOUISE: (*Laughing.*) Look at you. You should just see yourself. You just don't know what to think, do you, Mr *Enfant Terrible.*

KEN: I haven't been that for thirty years. (*He offers her a cigarette and she takes it.*)

LOUISE: Adult *ordinare*. I'm just giving you a hard time. Have a light, darling?

KEN: Of course.

LOUISE: So. What do you want?

KEN: I'm interested in your life, your work. Your beginnings as a dancer, your time on Broadway with Ziegfield Follies, your Hollywood films, your work with Pabst in Berlin. Why you walked away from films at the height of your career.

LOUISE: Why do you think?

KEN: That's what I'm here to find out.

LOUISE: You tell me.

KEN: I think you had integrity.

LOUISE: Maybe I was just bored.

KEN: I've read your magazine pieces about film acting, and the corruption of the Hollywood system – I think they're fabulous.

LOUISE: You're bullshitting me, darling.

KEN: I'm not! You're a very talented writer.

LOUISE: You slay me. (*Smiling.*) You really want to sit here for three days and talk to a mean old bag about her utterly, utterly, miserable life? Hm? I know what you really want.

KEN: What do I want?

LOUISE: You want *her*.

*LULU pops up over the headboard of the bed. She is wearing
a corset and transparent striped Victorian bloomers. She sits
on the headboard, her ankles crossed, inches away from
LOUISE.*

KEN: I don't know what you're talking about.

LOUISE: You do. She might live in your fantasy world,
sweetheart, but believe me, you don't live in hers.

KEN: Nonsense, darling.

LOUISE: I've been trying to kill her off for fifty years, and
everyone wants to bring her back to life.

KEN: Darling, you have to forgive people admiring you.
They can't help it.

LOUISE: But they don't exist to me.

KEN: But you exist to them. The entire western world has a
collective memory of your face – the face you see in
your mind when you think of the twenties. You embody
a time and place in history.

LOUISE: Yeah? Well, that's not *my* problem.

KEN: Some people wouldn't think of that as a problem.

LOUISE: You, maybe.

KEN: Darling, I think it's an honour. You're an icon.

LOUISE: An icon.

KEN: Yes!

LOUISE: Imagine this. At this moment, somewhere in the
world, someone you've never met, is obsessed with you.
They're thinking about you right now. They're looking
at a grimy old photograph of you that they ripped out of
a library book and keep folded up at the bottom of the
sock drawer. Their whole life revolves around meeting

you. They think, if only – if only the two of you could meet, you would suddenly know, somehow, that this was *the* person that the cosmos had created to make you complete! That kind of crap. Now, would you feel good about that? Would you feel safe?

KEN: But surely, darling, that is what it means to be a celebrity.

LULU crawls off the bed to kneel at KEN's feet. She rubs up against his leg like a cat.

LOUISE: No thanks, darling. I don't want to be a celebrity. Somebody that other people project their sick and unwholesome fantasies on? She's a light on the screen for chrissake! Emulsion in a few cans of disintegrating film. She doesn't exist!

KEN: But you do.

LOUISE: Even if she was real, she's dead. I killed her. I drank, smoked, and fucked her into oblivion, pardon my french. But you know what really stuck the knife in her, darling? I got old.

KEN: Now…

LOUISE: I got old. Face it, this face is fifty years older than the one you had in mind when you were outside my door. True or False.

KEN: Let's not talk about *her* any more. Let's talk about you.

LULU, hurt, looks up at KEN then exits.

You were born in Kansas, 1906.

LOUISE: Yeah. Like Dorothy.

KEN: Like Dorothy. (*Pause.*) A little girl plucked from the cornfields who, at the end of her trip to a magical world, finds that happiness was in her own backyard.

LOUISE: Not quite.

KEN: No?

LOUISE: I was thinking of a Dorothy who runs away from home at fourteen and lands in a goddamn magical world full of freaks who want to rob her. She is unable to worship those mighty men of power who she does not admire. And at the end of her usefulness to the cowards, the fools, and the heartless bastards, she limps into obscurity never to venture forth again.

KEN: I see.

LOUISE: Yes, I love that movie. Oh, you're disappointed.

KEN: I'm not disappointed.

LOUISE: You *are* disappointed. I should have said I like some deep movie.

KEN: And now, 'There's no place like home'?

LOUISE: Oh, please. That line nearly ruined it for me.

KEN: Let's talk about – your daily life.

LOUISE: Who'd want to know about that? I spend eighty per cent of my time in bed.

KEN: So do I.

Lights change as title slide comes up:

Rosebud

KEN sitting, legs crossed, notebook on his knee. He has a drink and a cigarette in one hand, pen in the other. LULU is revealed upstage. She is wearing a transparent version of Dorothy's gingham dress.

LULU: Whatcha doin?

KEN: Work.

LULU: Play with me.

KEN: Not tonight, darling. I'm busy.

LULU: Too busy for me?

KEN: Too tired.

LULU: Tired of me?

KEN: Just tired.

LULU: Then it must be time for bed. (*Moving in to him.*)
I know what you need. You need a little pick-me-up.
Hm? Then you'll feel more like your old self.
(*Whispering in his ear.*) More like your old, *old* self.

KEN: Piss off.

LULU: Don't you love me any more? That's it. You don't
love me anymore. You dislove me.

KEN: It's not that. Good heavens, what are you wearing?

LULU: Oh, no darling! You don't mean to say…you…you
…respect me? (*Swooning and shielding her eyes from the
light.*) Ohhhhhh. Ohhhhhh. I'm feeling faint! (*As if she can
see through her hand.*) Look! I'm disappearing! I'm
vanishing! Look at me! Look! Look! I'm melting!

She melts, and pounds the floor when he doesn't look up.

Look at me. Look! I'm dissolving! (*Her voice becomes faint,
'à la Camille'.*) Goodbye, darling! I'm fading away! (*A
couple of faint tubercular coughs.*) Goodbye… (*Croaks
hoarsely.*) Rosebud… (*She dies.*)

KEN looks up.

KEN: Still with us?

LULU: (*Sitting up.*) I'm better now. (*She flips through one of
his notebooks.*) What's this?

KEN: Notes for the profile. It could change everything.

LULU: How you feel about me?

KEN: Never, darling.

LULU: We'll see.

> *KEN returns to his work. LULU slithers over but he ignores her. She slithers in a position to be able to read over his shoulder. When KEN realises what she is doing, he covers the page with his hand.*

> *LULU climbs over his shoulder, on top of his book and onto his lap, looking up at him. After an exasperated pause, KEN gives in and kisses her.*

KEN: Don't force me to kill you in self-defence, darling.

LULU: It's the only way you'll get rid of me.

> *Lights fade. Title slide:*

Follies

KEN and LOUISE are looking at photos and clippings from a box, drinking and smoking.

LOUISE: Look. At. Her.

KEN: An angel whore.

LOUISE: Not good enough to be an angel, too dumb to be a whore. I mean, look where I'm spending my golden years. I was never any good at spoiling men.

KEN: Where is this?

LOUISE: Don't you know? That's Joe Zelli's in Paris, darling. I'm stewed in this one, all right. Oh, and look at that dress! Half naked in the afternoon!

KEN: I've never seen a photo with so much of the 'twenties in it. Who are all these gentlemen? Mobsters?

LOUISE: Ha, I don't know – oh, no, wait. I went to bed
   with him. And him. He gave me a silverfox stole and I
   let him take me to a tea dance just once. Oh, what a
   heartless racket. This one gave me a hundred bucks for
   the powder room.

KEN: I say. (*Picking up another photo.*)

LOUISE: He was a bastard. (*Looking at the next photo.*) My
   God! Is she ever sexy. Look at those gams!

KEN: Lyric.

LOUISE: They aren't that great.

KEN: The first time I saw you was when I was at Oxford in
   the 'forties, in a old *Photoplay* magazine, from 'twenty-six.
   You were in bed, just like this, when they photographed
   you. The reporter described you as 'So very Manhattan.
   Very young. Exquisitely hard-boiled… Her legs are lyric.'

LOUISE: Yeah, yeah. I never read anything written about
   me that didn't make me puke.

KEN: If she doesn't have *it*, I don't know what *it* is.

LOUISE: Who does? That's why they called it *It*.

KEN: The ability to project one's entire personality, one's
   soul, with a minimum of visible effort. High Definition
   Performance. That's why I love you, darling.

LOUISE: Shut up.

KEN: The jazz baby sophisticate.

LOUISE: You slaaaaay me, you just slaaaaaay me!

KEN: What? What did I say?

LOUISE: I didn't want that kind of life!

KEN: Well, then?

LOUISE: What?

KEN: What kind of life did you want?

LOUISE: Well, your life. I wanted to read books, and write, and be with brilliant people.

KEN: Not exactly the American Dream.

LOUISE: You got that right. Oh, everyone thought I was such a snob, reading Proust and Goethe between takes instead of the *Police Gazette*. They hated me and my superior attitude!

KEN: Must have been hair-raising to see the most beautiful woman of the twentieth century turning the pages of *Faust.*

LOUISE: Oh, yeah. You know, Mr Pabst moved to Hollywood from Berlin in the thirties to make a movie of *Faust* with me as Helen and Garbo as Gretchen.

KEN: Fantastic! What happened?

LOUISE: Hollywood wouldn't give him the money to do it, and certainly not with *moi*, so he went back to Germany to make films for the Nazis.

KEN: What a waste.

LOUISE: All I made after that was a couple of crap westerns. It was in the cards for us flappers anyway. Sex symbols were changing. You know, when Garbo arrived, oh! we were in despair!

KEN: She never did anything for me, darling.

LOUISE: Darling, Garbo was never meant for you, she was meant for *women.*

KEN: She did have the most thrilling walk. But she was much too perfect to be really…

LOUISE: Yeah. Real ice goddess. She made a pass at me once, at a party. My God, she was a terrific star. She was really gorgeous, really *knew* what she was doing. Know her?

KEN: Not really.

LOUISE: No. Who did? (*She unfolds a newspaper clipping.*)

KEN: Not much on there, darling.

LOUISE: That's in *Ziegfeld Follies.*

KEN: How did the cornfields produce that?

LOUISE: I do not know.

KEN: That's what the American male thinks is beautiful. Shiny things moving with mechanical precision.

LOUISE: You got that right.

KEN: There's something so sublime about the showgirl.

LOUISE: It was too, too divine. I was just nineteen in 1925. Me and Charlie swinging into the Lido, furs dripping off my shoulders. And I tell you, I was magnificent then. I had this lethal gold lace dress, terribly itchy but *divine*, and the dance floor cleared when we did the tango.

KEN: Charlie?

LOUISE: Oh it was marvelous. For two months, while he was opening *The Gold Rush*, two perfect summer months. It was like a fairytale. And he was like…an enchanted prince.

KEN: Chaplin.

LOUISE: You should have seen him then. He was just so clean, you know? Just perfectly made, and small, and glowing all over like a pearl. He had this thing around him. Even when he was asleep.

KEN: My. My.

LOUISE: And you must remember that at that time, he was the most famous man who ever lived. More famous than, say, oh…

KEN: Jesus Christ?

LOUISE: I heard there's this place on some island somewhere where they actually do worship him as a god, and I tell you, I would go there and be a disciple or whatever. He knew he was a genius who had created a great masterpiece – that must be perfect happiness, don't you think? Hey?

KEN: Yes. What?

LOUISE: What do you think happens when you get what you really want – your heart's desire? When you achieve perfect happiness?

KEN: You become impotent.

LOUISE: You maybe. Not for Charlie, that's for sure! Now, *he* was a very sophisticated lover. You can't imagine.

KEN: Can't I?

LOUISE: No.

KEN: You have to tell me about this, darling.

LOUISE: Oh, no no. So you can write me down and sell me to a dirty magazine for money? The unbelievable sexcapades of the wild Louise Brooks.

KEN: No. I wouldn't want to do that to you.

LOUISE: You will, though. (*Pause.*) You *will* want to.

KEN: You've lead a life of sexual integrity.

LOUISE: Listen to you! Sexual integrity. I like that. You naughty boy – you'll make me like myself.

KEN: You wrote that sexuality is the only key there is to truly knowing a person.

LOUISE: It's the only way to explain why people do unexplainable things.

KEN: Like throwing away careers? Burning bridges?

LOUISE: Oh sure. I did what I wanted. What anyone would do.

KEN: Not everyone does what they want.

LOUISE: No? Stupid everyone, then. Fine, what anyone would do, given certain opportunities.

KEN: Looking like that.

LOUISE: Well, sure. Being that young.

KEN: And famous.

LOUISE: And not caring a good goddamn for anyone.

KEN: You must have left quite a trail of broken hearts.

LOUISE: Ha! To break someone's heart you have to care, and I say, who cares?

KEN: That's what Lulu says.

LOUISE: Oh, yes?

KEN: Yes. In the film, Alwa says 'Do you love me, Lulu?' and she replies, 'I? Never a soul!'

LOUISE: Well, fancy that!

KEN: So what happened?

LOUISE: What?

KEN: You and...the Little Tramp.

LOUISE: Well, summer ended. You know. And he sent me a nice big cheque. Be a sugarpie and loan me a cigarette, will you? I'm out.

He does.

43

KEN: I have a confession. I once went to a costume party. I went. As you.

LOUISE: No!

KEN: Oh, yes.

LOUISE: Did anyone know who you were supposed to be?

KEN: They asked, of course, and I told them, 'Baden Powell.'

LOUISE: You lie!

KEN: I'd never lie to you darling. You'd find me out.

LOUISE: You're such a slut, darling.

KEN: I think we know who the slut is here.

LOUISE: You'd make one hell of an ugly woman.

KEN: Yes. (*Crossing back to LOUISE.*) But I really wanted to find out how it would feel.

LOUISE: To be a girl?

KEN: No, no, to be – oh, I don't know. (*Picking up another photo.*)

LOUISE: 'The Brooks Bob.' That's what they called it. I was in all the salon windows, everybody wanted it – the haircut my mother gave me on a kitchen stool back in Witchita. I made twenty-four films and my hairstyle is the one thing about me that will endure. Pathetic, isn't it?

KEN: You're were terribly 'in' in the 60's.

LOUISE: I'll come around again, no doubt. It's a comfort, really. No one knows who the hell I am, but I come back into vogue every fifteen years.

KEN: You're too much, darling.

LOUISE: What about you? What will you endure as? The man who said 'fuck' on TV? (*Pause.*) I was joking!

KEN: It's no joke.

LOUISE: Listen, you're a real success. You've written books. People care about what you think. Hell, you tell people what to think.

KEN: It's not the same as creating something new. It comes easily to some people. People who can walk in front of a camera, for instance, and create a work of art.

LOUISE: I never asked for it.

KEN: And I'll never achieve it.

LOUISE: Well, you can take it.

KEN: But I don't have what it takes to make it last.

LOUISE: 'It.'

KEN: That's it.

LOUISE: You know what Goethe said? He said that a man's life isn't important for what he leaves behind, but only if he acts and enjoys, and rouses others to action and enjoyment. Hey? That's just what you do.

KEN: Thank you.

LOUISE: To be a great person is the only work of art. (*She picks up another photo.*)

Photo slide shows a teenage Louise in a dancing costume, looking back over her shoulder.

KEN: What a wicked thing. A naughty altar boy.

LOUISE: That's when I was fifteen. Used to dance for Rotary.

KEN: God help us all.

Lights change. KEN sits on ottoman, with a drink and a cigarette, watching LULU. LULU is lying on her back, legs in the air, reading a very thick book.

Come on darling.

LULU: Did someone speak? Or was it the wind?

KEN: Come on.

LULU: Oh, it's you.

KEN: Yes, it's me. Come here.

LULU: You have time for me now, do you?

KEN: There's always time for you.

LULU: I thought you didn't want me anymore.

KEN: Of course I want... I need...

KEN pulls her around to straddle him, kissing and caressing her. She does not look up from her book.

What's that?

LULU: This?

KEN: Yes. What are you reading?

LULU: *A la Recherche du Temps Perdu.*

KEN: Ha, ha. Very amusing.

LULU: 'At the taste of the lime cordial-soaked madeleine, the past rose up in my mind like scenery at the theatre...'

KEN: (*Pushing her off.*) Oh no, now, look. Here's a magazine. (*Handing her one.*) Read that. Read *Vanity Fair.*

LULU: No.

KEN: Read a nice fashion magazine.

LULU: No Proust! Proust!

KEN: It doesn't look right on you.

LULU: Why?

KEN: It looks…

LULU: Cheap?

KEN: Oh, never mind.

LULU: Read it to me.

KEN: I'm busy.

LULU: Come on. Come on and read it to me.

KEN: Where are we?

LULU: (*Pointing to her place.*) Here. Here.

KEN: 'The time which we have at our disposal each day is
elastic. Passions expand it, those we inspire contract it,
and habit fills up the remains.'

LULU crosses her legs and rubs them together.

Don't do that, darling. You'll set yourself alight.

Title slide:

Occupational Hazards

*The film shows Schoen's first entrance, to tell Lulu he is getting
married. KEN is alone. He lights a cigarette. His breathing is slightly,
but noticeably, laboured.*

KEN: I spent my life taking people's breath away. Now it
appears I have to pay some kind of penalty.

*LULU enters, and she and KEN synchronise with the film
until the end of his monologue.*

My doctor made me a radioactive daiquiri and took
X-rays of my lungs. Two spreading elms lit by
moonlight, a few scattered leaves. He said it's time for

oxygen therapy. But I just can't wear that scuba gear. It just doesn't *go*. I've been advised to alter my lifestyle. But style *is* my life. Style before substance. Style before breath. By all means, Ken, continue to work, but indulge in pleasures other than smoking, drinking, amphetamines and sex. Anyone? I live in my head. I have installed four stalwart locks on its door, to be opened by four sacred keys. Cigarettes. White wine. Dexymyl. And masturbation. When you live in your head, darlings, you need these little things to help you face the mess inside. I need my keys to gain access, to work, but my weaknesses feed the disease. The emphysema... It's taken away the... I can't... I'm... I've lost a key. I'm locked out. I'm desperate to get back in, I must, I'm helpless, pounding on the door, peering through the mail slot, all the bills, contracts, queries about work I promised, piling up on the floor. I am breaking to pieces with anxiety, over-working and not working. The fear of creating, of not being able to create. Fear of never being able to begin. Fear of becoming incoherent, of losing my mind, of losing myself, my one work of art, the one most impermanent thing. Of disappearing without a trace.

LULU: Come on. Come on, darling.

Lying on her back, LULU puts her arms around his neck to pull KEN down, or herself up, to be kissed. The kiss occurs on the screen, but KEN closes his eyes and shakes his head.

KEN: I can't even enjoy enjoying myself any more.

Title slide:

Venus Flytrap

A photo slide shows a close-up of Louise in 'Pandora's Box', in her mourning dress, lifting her veil. LOUISE and KEN sitting together, looking at a photo.

KEN: Lulu.

LOUISE: Yeah.

They stare and smoke.

KEN: On trial for shooting her husband on her wedding day. That look. What were you thinking about?

LOUISE: What the hell do you think I was thinking about? I was thinking about what I was doing!

KEN: No, I know, darling, that's not what I mean. How can one look – it's like the rise and fall of civilization, darling. Right there. So innocent, so intelligent. But so devastating.

LOUISE: I look like that because I didn't know how to act.

KEN: Well if you weren't acting, that's you up there.

LOUISE: You know, if you don't have the technique to protect yourself, you burn straight into that lens. That's why Mr Pabst cast me.

KEN: Instead of a German actress.

LOUISE: He looked all over the world for somebody to play Lulu. But the German actresses were too, oh, whorish. Then he saw me in some pointless little movie, I was playing a bathing beauty, or somebody's bad little sister, whatever, and he knew that he'd found his Lulu.

KEN: They say Pabst's greatest artistic achievement was casting you and letting you make the film for him.

LOUISE: Who says that?

KEN: Film historians.

LOUISE: That is bullshit.

KEN: Fine. I say that. Nothing else he did came close to the two films he made with you. *Pandora's Box* is a masterpiece because of you, whether or not you knew what you were doing.

49

LOUISE: You don't understand anything. He was a genius. And I was a great disappointment to him. I refused to be a serious actress. I mean, Berlin in 'twenty-nine was just a hothouse of sex and fabulous parties, artist's balls, the works! You'd have loved it, darling, so debauched, just divine! It would have been irresponsible to be responsible. I was sleeping with the actor who played Jack the Ripper at the time, and to keep us from going to the nighclubs, Mr Pabst would lock me in my room at night.

KEN: Did it work?

LOUISE: The first night it did. What a tantrum I threw! I howled like the poor caged beasts in the zoo across the street. But the next night, it was straight out the window and down the fire escape. I was still drunk on horrid German champagne when they let me out in to morning to take me to work. But I could tell that I wasn't fooling Mr Pabst. And for the first time I started to feel – what was it?

KEN: Guilt.

LOUISE: Like I deserved to be punished. At first I thought it might be that I was in love.

KEN: With the actor playing Jack the Ripper.

LOUISE: No, with Mr Pabst. I couldn't pull one over on him, that's for damn sure.

KEN: You were Lulu to him, the Lost Girl. He wanted to save you.

LOUISE: Someone's always trying to save me. Makes them feel better about themselves.

KEN: Does it?

LOUISE: Doesn't it? All I know is I was just supposed to stand in front of the camera and have sex with everyone and they'd all drop like flies.

KEN: The venus flytrap.

LOUISE: Clever.

KEN: You reinvented film acting. Compete simplicity.

LOUISE: Yeah, whatever.

KEN: What was it like to work with Pabst?

LOUISE: Well, first of all, here was I, so holy, so fed up with Hollywood, in a country where I couldn't speak a word, and so happy. I trusted him completely. Mr Pabst really knew how to get – inside me, you know? When the camera was rolling, his voice was…like a conscience. It was, oh! How can I describe…very…

KEN: Intimate.

LOUISE: Oh, yes.

KEN: I hadn't thought of that, but of course – there'd be no need for silence on the set, so he could tell you what to do while the camera was rolling.

LOUISE: No, no. It wasn't about that. He did it to make me *feel* what Lulu felt. Like this.

The film shows the wedding night scene of 'Pandora's Box', with Schoen and Lulu in the bedroom, in which Schoen offers Lulu a gun to kill herself to 'save them both', but she accidentally shoots and kills him.

Look at you. You're radiant. You make the pearls jealous that circle your neck. Thank them, thank them, before you put them to sleep. Don't let them feel sad that they are not you. At last, alone, with him, this moment, this night. Why does he look at you that way? You've done nothing. No, his eyes are filled with fear. How can he be afraid of you, a child? Weren't you happy together a moment ago, drunk on champagne and dancing with your wedding guests? Your dress, your lovely dress, your wedding dress, so cool and white, remember last night how you secretly put it on, how it slid like a lover's hand over your skin and made you shiver.

In the film struggle, Lulu shoots Schoen.

What have you done, Lulu? What have you done? You never did a thing you didn't want to do. And in this second everything has changed for you forever. Look at him. What is that coming out of his mouth? *Das Blut. Das Blut*, Louise…

The film freezes with Schoen having fallen at Lulu's feet.

I slept with him that night. That was the single greatest performance I ever gave, the night I went to bed with him. And you know, the funny thing was – I knew it. At the time, I knew that I would never be as good again as on that night, when I felt like I could just…surrender, you know? When being lost was the most beautiful thing. You know that feeling?

KEN shrugs and smokes.

Mr Pabst wasn't the same with me after that night. Told me to clean up my act, that I deserved whatever I got. He said, 'Louissse, the story of Lulu is your story. You will meet the same end.' But you know, I didn't listen. It scared the hell out of me, so I didn't listen.

KEN: Did you?

LOUISE: What, sugar?

KEN: End up like Lulu?

LOUISE: Well, it's not like I read the script. It was a terrible flop. In America it just died, died on the vine. I swore I'd never see it. If I never knew what the end was, then I'd never meet it.

KEN: Lulu becomes a prostitute and a victim of Jack the Ripper.

LOUISE: Well, I knew I wound up with a knife in the vagina.

KEN: An unrepentant hedonist mustn't be rewarded.

LOUISE: But that *was* a reward for her. He was Jack the Ripper, for chrissake, he couldn't help but kill the thing he loved. And Lulu dies in the arms of her dream lover, a sexual maniac. What sweeter reward could there be for her?

KEN: Have you still not seen *Pandora's Box?*

LOUISE: In 1970, at a festival. Boy was I drunk! I could really drink in those days.

KEN: What did you think of it?

LOUISE: Well, Pabst was wrong about me, for once. I didn't end up like Lulu. I saved myself. And here I am, fifty years later, still alive.

KEN: No seductive killers lurking in the shadows ?

LOUISE: That was the last time I was out.

KEN: That was the last time you went to a film?

LOUISE: No, I mean *out.*

KEN: The last time you were *out?*

LOUISE: Yeah.

KEN: That was eight years ago, darling.

LOUISE: Yeah.

KEN: Get dressed.

LOUISE: Why.

KEN: Get dressed, we're going out to dinner.

LOUISE: No we are not.

KEN: Go get dressed. We'll go to the restaurant in my hotel. No, we'll go to that little place round the corner.

LOUISE: No.

KEN: Look, darling. It will be fabulous. We'll celebrate. We'll drink champagne. We'll just have a wonderful, wonderful time that we'll never forget.

LOUISE: What is there to celebrate?

KEN: You. The Profile. And I have some wonderful news. I'll tell you all about it over dinner. Where's your coat?

LOUISE: Tell me now.

KEN: Oh, that'll spoil it. Let's wait till we're there.

LOUISE: I'm not going anywhere.

KEN: Fine. I've been talking to a few friends of mine, film people but not Hollywood – New York people, people with integrity. You'd like them.

LOUISE: Well, good for you.

KEN: They're simply fascinated.

LOUISE: About what?

KEN: You. A film about your life. It's perfect. You'd have complete artistic control, I'd see to that. And with your permission, madame, I could supervise the script.

LOUISE: I don't believe this.

KEN: I know I shouldn't say this, but I'm just mad about you darling. I really think you are the most fascinating creature, and really – oh, so wicked – I just adore…

LOUISE: I see. You just want to make money off me. And when you're through with me you'll throw me right back into the gutter. (*She is finding it hard to breathe.*) No one's going to make a dime off of this old bag.

KEN: Forget it. If you don't want…

LOUISE: I'm the solution to all your problems, aren't I? Money? Writer's block? Or am I your newest sex toy? Are senior citizens the latest thing with all the really fashionable swingers?

KEN: I'm sorry.

LOUISE: You're sick!

KEN: Forget I said anything.

LOUISE: I trusted you. When I opened the door to you I thought, now, I could love this man. He could understand me. But you're just another opportunistic bastard. Get out.

KEN: Do you want some water? Have some water.

LOUISE: And now you've given me emphysema. Get out of here.

KEN: Should I call for help? I can get your neighbour.

LOUISE: Get out.

KEN: Please. Please be reasonable.

LOUISE: Get out.

KEN: Fine. (*He leaves without looking back.*) Goodnight.

Title slide:

Monster

KEN is sitting alone, sulking. He has one hand on his waist, and in the other he holds a highball glass and a cigarette. LULU is wrapped in a black silk sheet.

LULU: Darling?

> *KEN ignores her.*

> Come on, darling. Come on. (*No response.*) Darling? Darling? (*She shimmies in her shroud, coyly guarding what she has on underneath.*) I've got your favourite. (*Stamping her foot.*) Oh, come *on*, darling.

KEN: I have to work.

LULU: Have a look.

KEN: Would you be so kind as to leave me alone?

LULU: Have a look first. Have one little look. Then I'll go. I won't bother you again.

KEN: Just go. Just go.

LULU: Look first.

KEN: Excuse me. Can you tell me who is directing this fantasy sequence?

LULU: You are.

KEN: That's right, darling. So do go, now.

LULU: No.

KEN: (*Closing his eyes and covering his ears.*) Go.

LULU: Punish me!

KEN: No.

LULU: You'll want to. You'll want to when you see what I've got under here.

KEN: I can't. I'm not feeling well. I have to work. I have to work.

LULU drops the shroud. She is wearing Louise's bedjacket and holding a medical cane. She holds it jauntily at her hip, like Chaplin.

I can't ever, ever forgive you for that.

LULU looks at KEN long and sadly, then crosses, limping heavily on the cane, to the ottoman and produces a telephone. She sits, raises the receiver and dials a number as KEN watches.

The phone on Louise's bed rings. Lights up on her room. LOUISE picks up phone and hands it to KEN.

LOUISE: Hello? Hello?

LULU: Hello?

LOUISE: Who is this? Hello?

KEN wrestles the phone away from LULU, holding her back with one arm.

KEN: It's me. I'm sorry.

LOUISE: I thought you wouldn't want to talk to me again.

KEN: Of course I do.

LOUISE: I was – I was really just wicked to you. I didn't mean it. Come back.

KEN: Tomorrow.

LOUISE: Now. Come now.

KEN: Get some rest.

LOUISE: Mr Pabst was right about me.

KEN: What do you mean?

LOUISE: I'm just like her. Like Lulu. I knew it.

KEN: Nonsense.

LOUISE: I cut myself off from everything for fifty years, just to prove him wrong.

KEN: And he was.

LOUISE: No, he was right. This is the end of my little movie. And here you are, my Jack.

LULU hangs the phone up and strokes his hair as the lights fade.

Title slide:

Pandora

LOUISE in bed. KEN enters.

KEN: Hello, darling.

LOUISE: Oh, hello there.

KEN: I brought you a present.

LOUISE: Oh. *Tynan Right and Left.* How thoughtful. I don't have anything to give you. Except a drink. Come on, have a drink, darling?

KEN: Of course darling.

She pours him a drink and hands him a glass.

LOUISE: So. Let's just forget about my little outburst, shall we? We can still have a lovely evening. A lovely last evening together.

KEN: All right.

LOUISE: What do you want to do? Anything. Just pretend it never happened. Name it.

KEN: I don't mind.

Pause.

LOUISE: All right, then it's my turn to interview you. I've been blabbing on about myself for days and I don't really know a damn thing about you.

KEN: Fire away.

LOUISE: We'll start at the beginning. Where were you born?

KEN: Magdalen College, Oxford. 1945.

LOUISE: Let's see. That makes you…thirty-three?

KEN: Anything that happened before that is irrelevant.

LOUISE: Parents?

KEN: I'm a bastard, darling.

LOUISE: Genealogically or temperamentally?

KEN: I prefer to think that I'm artistic by temperament.

LOUISE: Don't worry. I always like the bastards best. I always had a passion for some kind of bastard. I didn't hurt your feelings?

KEN: No. I'm flattered.

LOUISE: Good. I'm improving. I was never any good at flattering men. Now, tell me about your family.

KEN: Wife, ex-wife. Three children. Mistress. Cat.

LOUISE: Oh, dear. Oh, no, you shouldn't have told me that. I shouldn't have asked. That ruins everything.

KEN: I'm sorry.

LOUISE: I *hate* cats.

KEN: Oh.

LOUISE: Marge says, 'Oh, Louise, you should get a cat!
They're no bother and they're such nice company!' Oh,
they're terrible. They never leave you alone. They lie on
your books when you're reading, ruin your work…
Ooooo touch me, pet me, I hate them! What's the matter
with you?

KEN: Nothing. It's…

LOUISE: What?

KEN: Oh, never mind.

LOUISE: I'm hardly in a position to judge other people's
morals. You can't have it both ways.

KEN: Oh, darling, I can think of at least a hundred ways of
having it.

LOUISE: So. Who are you going to 'do' next? Now that
you're finished with me.

KEN: I don't know. I have a lot of loose ends to tie up.

LOUISE: Before you go to Spain? (*Pause.*) You know, I've
never been there. I bet it's wonderful. Tell me what it's
like.

KEN: Oh, very arid.

LOUISE: Arid.

KEN: Lucid. Vivid. Sordid.

LOUISE: Torrid?

KEN: All the adjectives that end in 'id'.

LOUISE: It sounds sublime.

KEN: It is exactly that, like you. Too beautiful to fear the
consequences.

LOUISE: Sounds like our kind of place.

KEN: Come with me.

LOUISE: Me? To Spain?

KEN: Yes.

LOUISE: You're joking!

KEN: I'm not.

LOUISE: You're being cruel.

KEN: No, I mean it. Come to Spain. I rent a villa. There's plenty of room.

LOUISE: What on earth would I do in Spain?

KEN: Whatever you like. Write more articles. Read. Nap. Lounge. Wear a mantilla and danth the flamenco. No, a gypsy kerchief over your hair and gold hoops dangling from your ears.

LOUISE: I could tell fortunes and scare the hell out of everybody.

KEN: You'd look just like Marlene Dietrich in *Touch of Evil.*

LOUISE: That galloping cow? No thanks, darling.

KEN: Why do you say that?

LOUISE: Well, for one thing, she said to all the papers, 'Imagine Georgie Pabst choosing Louise Brooks for Lulu when he could have had me.' Oh she was a bitch.

KEN: She's actually a dear friend of mine, darling.

LOUISE: Isn't the world of famous people small? Everybody knows everybody. (*Pause.*) So. What did you do with her? Talk?

Pause.

KEN: We disappeared for three days together.

Pause.

LOUISE: Did you do it?

KEN: None of your business, darling.

LOUISE: Fuck you.

They smoke.

Truth or dare?

KEN: Dare.

LOUISE: Thought so.

KEN: So, what's the dare?

LOUISE: I'm sorry, darling, but the game is over for me once you state your preference.

KEN: All right. Truth, then.

LOUISE: Too late. (*Pause.*) You try me now.

KEN: But I know what you're going to say.

LOUISE: Try me. I might surprise you.

KEN: Well, then. Truth or dare?

LOUISE: Truth.

KEN: You see?

LOUISE: Go ahead. Ask me anything.

KEN: Really?

LOUISE: Anything. Shoot.

Pause.

KEN: I can't think of anything.

LOUISE: It's a good thing I didn't grant you three wishes.

KEN: All right. No matter how personal?

LOUISE: Anything.

KEN: You don't have to answer.

LOUISE: I will.

KEN: Do you ever have... Do you have any...fantasies?

LOUISE: Fantasies.

KEN: You know. Of a...sexual nature.

LOUISE: No.

KEN: No?

LOUISE: Never.

KEN: Never.

LOUISE: Well, I never needed any, did I?

KEN: How interesting.

LOUISE: You?

KEN: Of course. I'm Kenneth Fucking Tynan, darling. I'm the man who said 'fuck' on TV.

LOUISE: Now don't be like that.

KEN: Sorry. (*Pause.*) You really trust me to write about you?

LOUISE: You are the only one I trust.

KEN: I'm really hopeless these days.

LOUISE: Oh, give me a deadly sin any day over insipid hope.

KEN: The blancmange of human emotion.

LOUISE: I used to be quite an expert in sin, darling. Back before you were born. Now, let's see. Jealousy, avarice, greed...

KEN: Those two are the same. Covetousness.

LOUISE: Oh right. Gluttony. Anger. Is anger one?

KEN: I think it is.

LOUISE: Sloth. Look out for that one, darling. Envy. No, we had…

KEN: …Had that one. Pride.

LOUISE: That one's for me. One, two, three, four, five, six. There's one…

KEN: Starts with an 'L'.

LOUISE: Oh! Love!

KEN: Lust.

LOUISE: Whatever. You know, I don't think I loved any man. It was easy to give them up for the public library.

KEN: Ha.

LOUISE: I used to know lots of brilliant, brilliant men. I never found any show business person as sexually attractive as a really brilliant literary mind, you know what I mean? That's what I find really – oh, glamorous. I just don't get to meet brilliant people any more.

KEN: Is that so?

LOUISE: I miss that most of all.

KEN: I could introduce you.

LOUISE: You could, couldn't you?

KEN: Yes.

LOUISE: After the thing comes out.

KEN: Of course. Who would you like to meet?

LOUISE: Who do you know?

KEN: Well, everybody.

LOUISE: Such as?

KEN: I introduced Tennessee Williams to Ernest
 Hemingway and Fidel Castro.

LOUISE: Well, I'm so fucking impressed, darling, I can't
 tell you.

KEN: It's true.

LOUISE: Did I say it wasn't?

KEN: I know some people in Los Angeles who would love
 to meet you.

LOUISE: I think that California sun fries the brain. You
 should get out of there while you can. Move to New
 York. That's where you belong. You could be my
 manager. What do you think? You're the only one who
 could manage me.

KEN: The climate here is terrible for my bronchitis.

LOUISE: Look, I've got emphysema and I'm fine. (*She
 watches him open his cigarette case.*) You should really give
 that up, sugar. No, I mean it. First day of the rest of your
 life or whatever.

KEN: The effort of the resolution would leave no time or
 energy for anything else.

LOUISE: I'm supposed to quit, you know. This could be
 our last cigarette, right here.

KEN: I can just see the firing squad.

LOUISE: Picture me, blindfold, hands tied, up against the
 wall.

KEN: Hm.

LOUISE: Now stop! Your dirty mind!

KEN: Any last requests?

LOUISE: Have a light, darling?

They light up.

So, what do you say?

KEN: Maybe after I finish the article.

LOUISE: Promise me you will.

KEN: I will if you do.

LOUISE: When the article comes out.

KEN: Yes.

LOUISE: When's that?

KEN: Late spring.

LOUISE: This spring?

KEN: Seventy-nine.

LOUISE: That's over a year! Oh, that's fine. I can do it by then. Either that or I'll be dead. Now there's an idea. Could you write about me as if I was dead?

KEN: What about absolute truth and integrity? (*He gets up and picks up the phone.*)

LOUISE: What are you doing?

KEN: I have to get a cab. My plane leaves…

LOUISE: Get back over here, this instant. Come on. Sit here by me. Come sit next to Brooksie. (*He does.*) Look at those lovely hands.

KEN: (*Admiring them himself.*) Yes, they're very tenuous.

LOUISE: What a *thing* you are. Like a lovely peacock, all flash and crow.

KEN: Peacock is my middle name, darling.

LOUISE: Oh, I didn't mean it as an insult, darling, I meant…lovely things.

KEN: No, no. I mean Peacock is my *actual* middle name.

LOUISE: Oh. How truly bizarre. Maybe I'll change my name. What do you think. I can start over. How about June Caprice? That's good. Or Louise Lovely. Too vain. How about Lou Brou? Kind of Chinese.

KEN: Very Zen, darling.

LOUISE: Will you miss me when I'm gone?

KEN: Oh. Oh, of course. It'll be like losing a bit of myself.

LOUISE: But a little bit of me and you will always be together.

KEN: Yes.

LOUISE: In print. Where it counts. Where it lasts.

KEN: Yes.

LOUISE: What will you call it?

KEN: (*He touches her face as if drawing on Lulu's hair.*) 'The Girl in the Black Helmet.'

LOUISE: I like that. You understand me. I don't know if you know that, but I think you really do. Read to me, darling, before you go.

KEN: What shall I read?

LOUISE: (*Reaching for a book.*) This, this.

LOUISE opens the book to the right page. KEN puts his arm around her and she snuggles up with her head on his chest.

LULU enters, smoking, drinking, dressed in a long black negligé, an angel of death. She remains in the background.

KEN: My love is as a fever, longing still,
For that which longer nurseth the disease;
Feeding on that which doth preserve the ill,
The uncertain sickly appetite…

LOUISE: Go on. I didn't tell you to stop.

KEN: …The uncertain sickly appetite to please.
My reason, the physician to my love,
Angry that his prescriptions are not kept…
Oh, darling, I'm sorry, this is a bit much for me right
now.

LOUISE: Go on.

KEN: Er…desire is death…oh, dear…past cure…
And frantic-mad with evermore unrest;
My thoughts and my discourse as madmen's are,
At random from the truth vainly express'd;
For I have sworn thee fair and thought thee bright,
Who art as…

LOUISE: Oh, darling.

KEN: …Black as hell, as dark as night.

LOUISE: Lovely. Don't go.

KEN: I'll stay as long as you like.

*KEN strokes her hair as LOUISE falls asleep. KEN sits
with LOUISE in his arms until he is sure she is asleep. He
deliberates, then kisses her on the mouth. She remains asleep.
He rises, tucks her into bed, and turns to LULU. She doesn't
look at him.*

Look at you. You're radiant.

LULU: I'm drunk, darling. I'm drunk.

KEN: Let us always be drunk, darling. We shall sit in this room and be drunk and radiantly beautiful forever, living on wine and bread, and black coffee.

LULU: But you don't like your coffee black, darling.

KEN: But it looks divine.

LULU: Too, too divine. These books, this music. We'll be so *terribly* Bohemian

KEN: We'll live outside time. We will be always together, aspiring to be wonderfully alone.

LULU: We'll be perfectly unnatural.

KEN: Ordinary life is not our kind of thing. There will be no two –

LULU: No *ones*.

KEN: No two *ones* like us in history. Two beautiful, brilliant ones.

LULU: Sad. Careless.

KEN: Sad, careless radiant stars. Tragic.

LULU: (*Stuttering.*) B-but we won't know we're in a t-tragedy. We'll be alive like anyone else, buying groceries, making a meal, reading a book.

KEN: That, darling, *is* the tragedy. We won't know that we're living the same lives as boring, talentless, ordinary people.

LULU: We must try to forget them.

KEN: It will be very hard. Useless lives. Wasted lives. I'm terribly frightened of that kind of life. So we must squeeze life and enlightenment and pleasure out of every moment.

LULU: Darling.

KEN: I think I…

LULU: Yes, darling?

KEN: I'm going to say something important.

LULU: I'm ready darling.

KEN: I think I could become very fond of you.

LULU: Nonsense, darling. It's just that my teeth match your wound.

LULU drops her cigarette into her glass, and exits. In the film, we see Lulu's death scene from 'Pandora's Box'.

The film clip plays as KEN removes his jacket, unfolds a folding chair in the spotlight down centre where he began, and sits, alone. He looks very old and ill. He is not smoking.

LULU enters with a portable oxygen tank. She puts the clear blue plastic air tubing over his head with the cannula leading into his nostrils, running down to the tank. She reaches over his shoulders to tighten the tubing at his neck, like a necktie. She kneels at his feet and looks up at him.

KEN: I did renounce the world in favour of a worthless thing. A mistress, so elegant, so sublime, so demanding. So faithful to me, so intolerant of anything that was not her. This is my last cigarette. It's a very inferior brand. I bought it from a crooked cardiac patient for an exorbitant sum. How unfair that this should be the last. Its taste erases all the lovely ones before.

(*Caressing the handle of the oxygen tank.*) Isn't this obscene? It's even rather disgusting to me now. But I've been forbidden so I must. You understand.

KEN bends down as LULU gives him a light. He smokes, painfully. Each drag burns his lungs, and he rubs his chest.

You were so slender, so firm, with your paperwhite skin, your smoldering eyes. The more I yield to you the more you arouse me. My passion for you numbs my desire for anything else.

LULU places her head on KEN's lap and closes her eyes.

I wish I had a dozen of you in a platinum case. Multiples of you. Lined up absolutely. Restrained with a clip. A sublime row of chorus girls, each identical, each one ready for me, begging to be the one I'll choose, the one I'll caress.

KEN rises and walks towards the screen. The image of LULU appears again as at the start of the play.

How poignant our short time together. How delightful to have killed a little time with you.

Lights fade. The film clip ends. Blackout.